An introduction to
Lectio Divina

Seeking
GOD
in
Scripture

Steele Hartmann OSCO

COVENTRY
PRESS

Published in Australia by
Coventry Press
33 Scoresby Road
Bayswater VIC 3153

ISBN 9780648861232

Scripture quotations are from the ESV® Bible (The Holy Bible, English Stan-
dard Version®), copyright © 2001 by Crossway Bibles, a publishing ministry of
Good News Publishers. Used by permission. All rights reserved; and from The
Jerusalem Bible © 1966 by Darton Longman & Todd Ltd and Doubleday and
Company Ltd.

Catalogue-in-Publication entry is available from the National Library
of Australia http://catologue.nla.gov.au

Cover design by Ian James – www.jgd.com.au
Text design by Coventry Press
Set in EBGaramond

Printed in Australia

Contents

Introduction

This God whom we seek, we Christians call the Most Holy Trinity. Sadly, many know this title only as reference to a difficult dogma at the centre of our faith, which can be simply put as: One God in Three Persons. This is the only simple part about it, for the doctrine of the Trinity is rather intellectually challenging. But it is useful to remember that doctrine follows experience, and that behind the doctrine of the Trinity lies the Christian experience of our God. It is perhaps best, then, to leave the dogma to the theologians, and for us to look behind the doctrine to the experience.

When Saint Paul speaks of his experience of God, he speaks of 'when God was pleased to reveal his Son in me that I might preach him among the Gentiles' (Galatians 1:16). The experience, then, is not some private indulgence, but for a purpose. So, Paul describes himself as Christ's servant (Galatians 1:10), as an apostle (Galatians 1:1), which means one who is sent. His understanding of the experience is in terms of 'Son', which fits his experience of being sent. For Christ, who is the Son, said of himself: 'I have come to do the will of the one who sent me' (John 4:34; 5:30).

In the Prologue to his Gospel, St John reminds us that 'No one has ever seen God; it is the only Son, who is nearest the Father's heart, who has made him known' (John 1:18). So the experience of

Son is a revelation of God, or better, the experience of one doing the will of God is a revelation of God. So, Jesus, the one who does the will of the one who sent him, says to us: 'To have seen me is to have seen the Father' (John 14:9). In the Gospels, his fellow Jews reject Jesus because he claims to be God's Son. He says to them, 'The works my Father has given me to carry out, these same works of mine testify that the Father has sent me... believe it on the evidence of this work, if for no other reason' (John 5:36; 14:11). It is the doing of God's will that reveals the Son in whom the Father is made known. Our experience of God, then, comes in terms of knowing God's will and doing it, and it is the doing that makes God known. This we are all sent to do; we are all called to be apostles. (John 17:6-8; 20:21) Our quest, then, is at heart a quest to know God's will and to do it. Doing this we will make God known.

It was St Paul's experience that 'to will good works is present in me, but to do them is not. I do not do the good I want to do, but I do the evil I do not want' (Romans 7:18-19). If we are honest, this is our experience, too. As Jesus said to the Jews who refused him, so he says to us as we are: 'But you, you put into action the lessons learned from your father. ... The devil is your father, and you prefer to do what your father wants' (John 8:38, 44). A son reveals who his father is in what he does; it is the doing that reveals. Left to ourselves, we have an impossible task to perform, for in our doing we cannot hope to reveal God. Along with Mary, we can only say to God, 'How can this be?' (Luke 1:34) and his answer is the same, 'The Holy Spirit will come upon you, and the power of the Most High will cover you with its shadow... for nothing is impossible to God' (Luke 1:35, 37). Like Mary, ours is to believe and step out in faith, and not to be put off by our present seeming inability. (See also Romans 4:18-22; 8:24-25.)

This Mary says to us, 'Do whatever he tells you' (John 2:5). In St John's Gospel, Jesus says to us, 'The Holy Spirit, whom the Father will send in my name, will teach you everything and remind you of all I have said to you' (John 14:26). In this light, we can see that the Gospels – and Scripture more broadly – is itself the work of the Holy Spirit, and that is why we hold their stories sacred: they tell what Jesus said to us, they tell us of God's word to us. This Jesus said to us while he was still with us, 'I still have many things to say to you but they would be too much for you now. But when the Spirit of Truth comes he will lead you to the complete truth, since he will not be speaking as from himself but will say only what he has learnt... All that he tells you will be taken from what is mine' (John 16:12-13).

This Holy Spirit does not reveal anything new to us, but will reveal to us the something more that is already there in what Jesus, God's word, says to us. This Jesus speaks to us in parables; it is not always immediately clear what he is really saying to us. He merely says to us: 'Listen anyone who has ears' (e.g. Matthew 11:15). We who seek to know God's will and do it must, then, start by listening: before we can be apostles, we must first be disciples. That is why for monks, Lectio Divina – that slow, meditative reading of Scripture – is their principal form of prayer. For in so doing, we allow the Holy Spirit to whisper in our ear, so to speak, and reveal to us what Jesus is saying (cf. Galatians 1:11-12). In this we imitate Mary, Christ's first disciple, of whom it is said: 'As for Mary, she treasured all these things and pondered them in her heart' (Luke 2:19, 51). And she did this especially when she did not understand: How can this be? (Luke 2:50)

Over time, in this process of patient listening, the word slowly begins to take flesh in us (John 1:14) and becomes flesh of our flesh (Genesis 2:23), and we begin to do what he tells us: we embody the word, if you like. When we find that we do start to keep his word (John 14:23), 'without effort, as though naturally, from habit, no longer out of fear of hell, but out of love for Christ, good habit and delight in virtue', then we must know that the Holy Spirit has indeed come upon us (*The Rule of St Benedict* 7:67-70). For we know what we can do, and that this can be none of our doing – along with Mary, we can only praise God: 'My soul glorifies the

Lord... for the Almighty has done great things for me' (*The Rule of St Benedict* Prologue: 29-32; Luke 1:46ff). In this experience of doing God's will (John 16:14-15; 14:23), under the influence of the Holy Spirit, we will reveal who our Father is – and indeed know who our Father is, for this Spirit will have us cry out: 'Abba/Father!' (Romans 8:15).

When this Spirit comes upon us, like Jesus, in our doing, we will experience our God as Father and ourselves as Son/Daughter – brothers/sisters and co-heirs with Christ (Mark 1:10-11; Romans 8:29). In our doing his will, we will reveal the God who is our Father by showing ourselves as Son/Daughter –then we shall do what we were sent to do; then we shall be what we were made to be: images of God in this world, and we shall be able to say along with Jesus, 'To have seen me is to have seen the Father' (John 17:6; Genesis 1:26-27; John 14:9).

The will of the Father being done is the Son; what enables is the Holy Spirit. This is the Christian experience of God. Christ has sent his Holy Spirit upon us all: we can all aspire to this experience! In so doing we will be taken into the Trinity as sisters and brothers of the Son. As St Paul puts it: 'For in this hope we are saved' (Romans 8:24). But first we must listen (*The Rule of St Benedict* Prologue 1:1).

It is this listening that we want to examine in looking at Lectio Divina, for it is more about listening than about reading. But before so doing, pause for a moment and look back over this introduction, for it is the fruit of my Lectio; I gathered it from my prayer. Notice all the Scripture references. Note that they do not all come from the same place, but from various and diverse sources scattered throughout the Bible – and yet I rub them all together, like so many separate strands spun together that go into making a rope. Not that this is the purpose of Lectio, for it has no purpose except converse with God. As you can imagine, the more familiar we become with Scripture, the 'better', the more satisfying, it becomes as an exercise in prayer.

In this book, I hope to give you some idea of what Lectio Divina is, to look at it as an art, a skill, that can be learned, and so, perforce, I will try to break it up into its various parts that we might understand it better and so learn the skill more easily (not that, in our experience of this prayer, we do consciously move from one stage to the next; it's just a useful way of looking at the form of the prayer). I will look at some differing ways that Lectio is practised, and share with you what I do when I pray the Scripture – always mindful that there is no one way, no 'right' way, no 'better' way of praying Scripture; there is only the way that works for you.

Lectio is more about a relationship with God in Christ than about reading, and so, just as in any relationship, there are and will be times when we don't/won't/can't talk to each other – and so I will look at the difficulties we might encounter in our discipleship of Christ as we sit at his feet. It is a great way to pray, which I recommend to you all.

Lectio Divina

As we begin, there is first a need to point out that we are embodied spirit. We have physical needs and spiritual needs: the need for food, the need for shelter and clothing, our various emotional and psychological needs, our need to love and be loved, and all the other needs of our spirit, our spiritual needs. Our needs need to be met, else we suffer (perhaps even die) – as, for example, if our need for food is not met, we starve and our body begins to waste away. Similarly, if our spiritual needs are not met, then we starve spiritually and our spirit starts to waste away. So, then, as part of our spiritual diet, we need to pray, especially those of us who are single.

Lectio Divina is an ancient tradition – coming ultimately out of our Jewish heritage, which had a love for and celebration of the written word of God. 'Lectio Divina' means 'spiritual reading', but it is more than just a mere perusal of spiritual books. It is a reading that seeks not information or even spiritual knowledge. Lectio, as it is more usually called, is about a relationship with God. Through our reading, we seek to meet the God within, between, and behind the lines. Our Jewish forebears in the faith had the notion that, when they heard the Ten Commandments being read out, they were having the same experience as those gathered there on Mount Sinai, that they were therefore in some way present there with them on the Mount, hearing what they heard and adding their 'Yes!' to the assent given to the Covenant with God, that they were one with all of God's People.

This notion was extended to whole of God's word, as found in Scripture, so that to hear Scripture being read out was to experience God speaking. It is this that our ancient tradition of Lectio Divina seeks to hang onto. Lectio, then, is more to do with listening than about reading as such. And our listening is our way of entering the Presence to hear. To the extent that we hear the Lord in his word, receive it into our being, we participate in God. This demands a certain level of faith: we have to believe it is God's word we encounter, believe that God is present in his word, and believe that this God wants to speak to me; we have to believe it is God who speaks when we hear.

Lectio and Discipleship

For us Christians, Jesus is the word. He is the revelation of God made manifest; he is God's word to us incarnate, in the flesh. This Christ is God's word, the word to which we must listen. The relationship we seek with God in and through Scripture, then, becomes for us, first and foremost, a relationship with Christ. But it is not just any relationship. It is a relationship in which God in Christ speaks first while we listen, only then may we respond. This relationship materialises in Christ's call to discipleship.

In ancient times, the disciple would sit at the feet of the Master. The Master would speak, and the disciple would listen. This is the essence of Lectio; through/in our reading, this is what we seek to do. Through it, in it, we sit at the feet of our Master, asking him for a word of life that we can take into ourselves, put it into practice, and live. Lectio is our way of discipleship of Christ, our way of sitting at his feet and listening.

To do Lectio properly, then, means we must be willing to be instructed, be willing to abandon our own judgments and preferences. In ancient times, to listen meant to hear and obey. Obedience is the appropriate response of a disciple. Benedict refers to it as: 'The labour of obedience which will bring you back to him from whom you had drifted through the sloth of disobedience'. There is a 'doing' aspect to Lectio, a labour; we must expect it is going to cost us effort. This 'labour of obedience' follows Benedict's injunction: 'Listen, my son/my daughter'. The basic vice of those who are disobedient, those estranged from God our Father, is the laziness of not listening. Such was akin to idleness. So, Benedict's remedy for those who will not listen/will not read/are lazy is work/manual labour! At least then one is not idle, idleness being the enemy of the soul (*Rule of St Benedict* 48:1). Lectio, then, is a work, one of the good works, one of the daily activities of a monk.

When we first start off, we usually just simply try to put into practice what we read there in the Gospels and in the Scriptures more generally. As disciples, we need and we want to respond, so we try to live in accord with Christ's teachings. But we soon discover there is more to following Christ than just obeying orders. The Bible is not a simple document. It was written over a long period of time. It was written by many different authors. It was written a long time ago. It was written as God's word to circumstances not our own. So, at times it can seem unclear, at times it can seem contradictory, at times it can seem like just so much nonsense. But just as it is hard to have a relationship with a person from a different culture – unless we take time to get to know them, to understand their customs, presuppositions and prejudices – so too with Christ.

Christ is God's word to us, but a word made incarnate in another culture very different to our own, in another time very different to our own. For us to make any sense of this word to us, we must first try to translate it into a word we can understand. To do this is not always easy, though in this we are aided by the many different translations of the Bible, a comparison of which will yield the many shades of meaning that surround the words of the Bible in their original context. Here, too, we can gain considerable help from biblical dictionaries and commentaries, and in annotated Bibles we can discover the many implicit references to other biblical texts that colour and shape what is being said.

As we become more familiar with Scripture, we begin to realise that a simple fundamentalism, which tries to simply apply what is literally said, just simply does not work: the customs and practices of a people from the distant past often do not and will not carry the meaning they once did when taken out of context and artificially grafted into our modern culture. Then, too, our modern world is vastly different from the ancient world. Things that confront us now were not even dreamed of in earlier times. Simply put, there is much in our modern world that the Bible just simply does not address. Thus do we discover that Scripture, God's word, is very much an incarnate word, a word subject to the limitations of finite being, of being finite.

Yet we are called to be Christ's disciple here in our modern world; we can be nowhere else. As we struggle to live according to Christ's teaching, we find ourselves wondering what Christ would do in our situation. Thus do we find ourselves desiring to know Christ, the person, more and more. We want to know him, to become so infused with his Spirit that his Spirit will be the source of all we do. Only then will we know how Christ would live and act in our world, only then will we know what to do to live as Christ did, for we will have put on the mind of Christ. This was the ancient aim of the Master/Disciple relationship. What was important was not so much the content taught, but the relationship, that prolonged contact whereby the disciple absorbs the spirit and style of the Master and so becomes just like the Master, or perhaps better, becomes the Master – where Master and disciple are one. This is the goal in Lectio. Our Lectio will be complete, will be successful, when we have become like Christ, become another Christ – so that, in our doing, we proclaim: 'To have seen me is to have seen Christ', so much so that, for another, an encounter with us will be as an encounter with Christ, where we shall be the icon of Christ/be his representative for the seeker of truth, where we shall be the servant for those in need, the friend of the lonely.

Lectio a Skill

Lectio is an art, a skill. That means it can be learned, and that its practice can improve over time as we hone our skill. To understand the basic elements of this skill it is helpful to look at how reading/Lectio was done in more ancient times. Few in olden days were literate, yet they heard God's word – in the liturgy, in refectory reading and Chapter talks. They would also receive a word, which was often a word of Scripture, from Spiritual Fathers and Mothers. The wealthy, and so too their household, would pay people to read to them. Reading had about it an aural aspect: the word was heard; reading as listening was real. Then, those who could read usually did so aloud. Reading, as an activity, was a physical one, involving lips, tongue and ears. Some feel we should not lose this element of physicality and suggest that we sub-vocalise as we read, so that we can 'hear' in our minds what is said as we read, or perhaps even read quietly aloud to ourselves. This would have the added benefit of helping keep distractions at bay. Further, it would slow down our reading, helping us to remember.

This, though, cannot be pushed too far, as Lectio really only came into its own as a prayer form with the shift to silent reading. Silent reading impacts on a person's internal dialogue. The reader now thinks the thoughts of the divine author, but now heard within the self as an active part of the dialogue. In this way, God now can/does speak to me personally and interiorly, in place of my own thoughts and in the place of my own thoughts. This, then, obliges me, the reader, to revise my (fixed? biased? narrow?) views on things in accordance with the message of the text, and which will then impact on how I act.

In this way, the gap, which usually separates the book and the reader/the self and the other and keeping me critically safe from undue influence, is bridged. In this way do I 'put on the mind of Christ.' In this way I am moved to conversion. St Bernard saw this use of our internal dialogue as the best preparation for contemplation. For instance, in a text that speaks of, say, God's love, of God loving me, we can see how it is, in hearing this and knowing it within ourselves, that we might begin to respond accordingly. Or it might be a passage from Christ's Passion, and so we might be moved by compassion and/or compunction. Thus is the affective engaged; thus it is another element in the process of Lectio Divina. (We can see in this how incredibly careful we need to be in our choice of what we read in Lectio.)

In oral cultures, memory is greatly valued and so we can also expect memory to have a great role in Lectio. In ancient times, books were scarce. This meant that, in the early times, Lectio was more often an exercise of memory than of actual reading; rather than reading, it was more hearing with the 'ear of the heart' as they remembered; memory was their book. A certain interiority, then, is characteristic of Lectio. Then, too, prayer was seen as the response to God's word. When coupled with the injunction, 'Pray without ceasing', this meant a need to listen without ceasing. So, people were encouraged to memorise Scripture that it may be continually recalled – wherever one may be, whatever one may be doing – that they may constantly respond/answer with brief prayers.

Our slow repetitious reading puts the reading into our memory where it will aid our prayer. There it will come into play by working/challenging/influencing our behaviour – when it does this we can be sure that we have welcomed God's word into our hearts; Scripture is only known when it is lived, when it is translated into our own lives. We read to evangelise our lives – if our reading has no effect, then we are just indulging ourselves in some devotional self-indulgence. What does not enter/is not retained cannot be recalled, what is not recalled cannot challenge/change – always mindful that this is a fruit of Lectio and not its purpose, which is always and only ever an encounter and converse with God.

In days long ago, books were rare and very expensive. Books were hard come by, and gaining access to them was not easy. That monks in those times spent so much on books (not only in terms of time copying and of money spent, but also in terms of all it took to ensure their preservation) testifies to how essential they considered Lectio Divina to be, for this was the major use for their books. Because of the expense, only books considered to be of value were copied, and so kept in circulation. Books, then, were valued, not just because of their great cost, but also because of what they contained. Book were read, not as some nice idle pastime, but because they were worthwhile. One read with purpose, expecting to get something out of it; one expected to learn something from a book. Thus, a person would read with openness. In our Lectio, we need to read with just such an open expectation; this is essential. This will guide our choice of what we read, for not all books are suited to being read so uncritically.

Books, being rare, were read and reread – so much so that people would know whole slabs by heart. As they read, this known and familiar material would readily come to mind as associations formed. These, then, would influence what was being read. This ability to recall other texts of Scripture and let it influence what we read is also an essential element in Lectio. Our Lectio gets better as we become more familiar with Scripture. Because they had few books, readers had no access to any reference material which might help explain something they did not understand. Instead they had to ponder on and puzzle over the text as they read till at last they came to some understanding. This pondering of the word is another essential element in Lectio, for as we have seen Scripture itself is not always straightforward reading, containing as it does words and phrases whose meaning have been lost in time. Further, Scripture is about God and so it is shrouded in mystery. If we are to understand we will have to ponder. This pondering will further cement the text into memory, making it available for later.

Our reading, then, has about it a physicality, involving eye, ear and lips, and memory. Coupled with this is its calls for an open expectation by and through which we can encounter the God who speaks and to whom we can respond. There is a real sense in Lectio in which we do come physically into the Presence of God where a two-way conversation can take place: God speaks, we listen, and we respond – harking back to the Jewish experience on Mount Sinai that was mentioned earlier.

Lectio is Not

There are some 'NOTs' about Lectio. Lectio is NOT an exercise in information gathering; it's not that kind of reading. Lectio is NOT a form of entertainment; we should not expect to see some kind of spiritual fireworks. If this is what we expect, we are bound to be disappointed. Rather, Lectio is a sober, long-term thing – there will be no immediate gratification, no immediate improvement in our lives (only time will reveal the change). Nor will our reading bring us to any sudden revelations (such are rare). Rather, we will see glimpses along the way as we gradually come to see things in a different light, the light of Christ Risen. Then, Lectio is NOT an exercise as in something that has to be done, a duty. If we see it as a duty, we are less likely to persevere in it.

Rather, Lectio is prayer, intimate prayer, where we take God's word into ourselves and let it influence us. It is a technique of prayer and a preparation for contemplation. It is a way of finding God. This we should want to do; this we should be eager to do. This is the test Benedict uses for admission to his school of the Lord's service: Does the novice truly seek God? And a tool Benedict gives us, to aid us in our endeavour, and which we must learn to use, is Lectio.

Lectio and the Spirit

In our seeking, we need to admit that we don't know the way, that we need a guide. This means we need to be willing to be led. Here our Lectio will help: the sacred authors will lead us to the God in Jesus. We need to be open to their guidance in a spirit of trust and confidence. Further, as it is prayer, we need to admit we don't know how to pray (properly/adequately/well – there is always something unsatisfying about our prayer). St Paul teaches us that, though this is so, the Spirit prays in us anyway. Our Lectio is a way of opening to this Spirit. As a method of praying, Lectio aims to develop a habit of prayer, of spending some time each day with the Lord, listening to him and responding to him, growing more like him in mind and heart, and letting him guide us more practically each day. Jesus promised us that the Holy Spirit who would teach us all things and remind us of all that he has said – this is what happens in Lectio; Lectio is co-operating with this Holy Spirit, a listening to his voice. This Holy Spirit is just as active today when we read the Scriptures as he was in their composition in days long ago.

Lectio as One Way to Pray

It is worth noting here that, while Lectio is a way of praying, it is only ONE way of praying. There is no 'right' way to pray, no 'better' way to pray. There is only the way that works for you. While my aim is to encourage you to see Lectio as a good and excellent way of praying and to try it, it is NOT my intention to say that this is THE WAY you must pray. Further, there is no one way to pray Lectio, for there are probably as many variations on how to do it as there are practitioners of it. What I will put forward are only suggestions. Each person must develop their own way of doing Lectio. It is, after all, a conversation, and just as there is no one way to converse, we each of us will speak to God in Christ in our own way, which is personal to us.

It is also good to speak here of changing how we pray. In the course of our lives we will change how we pray. How we pray as a child is not how we pray as an adult; how we pray as a young adult will not be how we pray when we are old. Many do little work on their spirituality and their prayer-life once they leave school and childhood, and probably most will not look to pray – until struck by some crisis. Then it is too late to learn how to pray. All they will have in their time of need are the words of a child, and these they will find childish and unsatisfactory, and they will be left feeling abandoned by God. (The reality is, though, it is they who had abandoned God... long before this time of need.)

We do need to develop our prayer as we grow. We may find, as we go along, that we do pray well, and this may continue for some time. But there does come times when our prayer seems no longer to work. If this is more than just a 'dry period', which inevitably and periodically punctuates everyone's prayer life, if we are truly in need of a new way of praying, we must not just simply jettison all that we have done previously. How we used to pray has sustained and nourished us spiritually up until now; it will continue to do for a little while longer as we explore new ways to pray. In the transition we should keep doing what we have always done, only abandoning our previous practice when it begins to impede us as we move into the new way, which we have found to be attractive and which seems to be working for us.

Change is inevitable. It may be destabilising and uncomfortable, but it is not to be feared. It does not mean that something has gone wrong. When we have to change, all it means is that what sustained us up until now is no longer adequate for the journey that lies ahead. There is no fixed way to pray; we can give ourselves permission to change. Lectio is a good adult way of praying, for it implies a whole process, a way of spirituality. It is a simple, innate way of spiritual life and growth. It is a guide to living. It will help fan the sparks of our fervour, and draw us out of ourselves to live more unselfishly. Lectio will help us to live, which is what we all seek to do and have to do.

Lectio and Faithfulness

There are a few other qualities we need to bring to our Lectio. We must be mindful that we do not know all about God. Thus, we do need to sit and listen. Because we meet God in and through

Scripture/God's word, and because we have been exposed to the Scriptures over a long period – if nothing else, every time we attend Mass they are read to us over and again in an unending cycle – we need to beware a boredom that say to us: 'I've heard all this before'. We must remember that we are not reading for information – that we have heard it before does not matter, for we are meeting a person, a person we are getting to know and with whom we are becoming familiar. We need to be open to meeting the person of Christ.

What deafens our hearing, what prevent us meeting, are all our old attitudes and prejudices (and which are masked by our boredom) – much in the same way as our prejudices prevent us from meeting people from other cultures and other races. Our fears, our prejudices, our selfishness and our self-centredness will stop us from hearing God in Christ speaking to us. What we will find, though, if we are willing to be a little open, is that God's word will start to challenge these very attitudes, opening us a little more, and we will begin to see in a new way. This we can find disturbing and unsettling, for it will move us out of our comfort zone demanding now that we do things differently. This is the Holy Spirit driving us. We do not always appreciate this, preferring to remain as we are (it's easier!). Here our resistance to God's word may begin to appear: we might find ourselves beset by distractions, feel disappointed/discouraged, find ourselves cutting corners and investing less in reading, feel bored/irritated/restless (want to be doing something else), find it all very tedious, feel God to be absent.

This resistance can even contribute to the dry spells we experience in our prayer. Here it can sometimes be helpful to have the assistance of a spiritual director, someone to ask the awkward questions, which will help us come to recognise our fears, prejudices and all that block us — so do we grow in self-knowledge, and also to challenge us when we refuse to see that our behaviour is at variance with what we are saying in our prayer and so in need of reform. We need to be conscious of our shortcomings and therefore conscious of our need to change; this cultivates our desire for conversion. There is much in us that resists God's word; this is part of our truth. When our resistance begins to surface, we can feel we are drifting away from God, that we can't hear him anymore, and we are tempted to give it all away. It is only persistence that wins through here. It does not mean that Lectio is not a good thing to be doing. What it calls for is trust: that God knows what he is doing, that God will leads us to good times again, that we are growing in God.

We also need to bring fidelity to our Lectio because Lectio, as a skill, is something that gets better the more we do it. This means, as with learning any skill, that when we first start off we will do it poorly. We just have to go through this if we are to become proficient at it. It is only a commitment to doing it that will carry us through here. In contrast to this, in our first fervour we usually start off all enthusiastic. This enthusiasm is part of the lubricant that helps us get through the learning period. But this soon gives way to a more seasoned composure, where the emphasis is on faith and fidelity, where we just have to simply go with our belief that Lectio is a good thing to do and stick with it, trusting that God will do his part. Again, the challenge here will be to remain faithful, to remain open to God's shaping word.

Then, too, life these days is very busy – there is any number of reasons why we should be doing something else. Prayer is very acquiescent: to any urgent request it will readily give way. Good excuses may absolve us of any blame, but they don't help us achieve our goal (this applies to anything, and not just to doing Lectio each day). Unless we give prayer a priority and commit to it, it will not happen. We need to define ourselves as one who meets the Lord daily in Lectio. This will keep us returning, even if we occasionally miss.

Further, we are aiming to learn how to live. We believe we will achieve this by following Christ's teaching, by conforming ourselves to the pattern of the Gospels. This presupposes some attempt to live it, to put it into practice. This doesn't just happen, but takes time as we come to understand and see more clearly. Our many attempts to reform – to do as the Gospel seems to demand – will fail. It is only when we come to see and understand what God's word really means AND means to me – that is, to see and understand how I can embody the Gospel – that we will be able to take it on board. Only a willingness to sit –perhaps for a long time – with the discomfort of the challenge will bring us to this clarity. This will only happen if we allow ourselves to be constantly exposed to God's word and the call inherent in it; I must let God's word address my situation continually; I must read regularly.

Our faithfulness, then, becomes the concrete expression of our willingness to reform our lives, our ongoing 'Yes!' to God's plan for us, our assent to being made anew in the likeness of Christ — though it may initially feel like being unmade, for we first need to be pruned and have our roots dug around before we can bear fruit. Here, though, we need to be mindful that Lectio is not meant to be part of a self-improvement course. Our self-improvement is more a by-product of this relationship, is part of our response as a partner in this relationship, as we let Christ, the one in this relationship with whom we let ourselves be intimate, influence and shape our attitudes, values and behaviour.

Lectio and Patience

Then, as a companion to faithfulness, we will need patience. Being finite, we are subject to time. It takes us time to do anything. It takes time to go anywhere, even to enter sacred space. It takes time for spiritual things to rise up for us to see them. Sometimes it can even take time, perhaps a long time, for us to see the connection of the word with our lives, to see the challenge/the call to reform in it. Then, for us to change in a way that will be lasting, this also takes time. At first, we may rush into a massive program of self-improvement, but we will probably not succeed because the sheer effort to maintain it is too great. When we don't have the energy for it, our old ways reassert themselves and so we slip again. Thus do we come to know our major failings, those things which constantly bring us undone.

It is these 'demons' we need to expose to God, and not keep hidden, for only God can drive them out; this is what reform/repentance is all about. We need first to see the truth of our being: our fragmentedness, our lack of integration, our lack of wholeness, our dissatisfaction with the shabbier side of our lives – all those things which we do not like to admit about ourselves, which we push aside because to confront, perhaps even just to look at them, is too painful, too embarrassing, too messy, or too uncomfortable, and so they remain unchallenged. Lectio will bring us face to face with this truth of our being, but it will take time for us to let our barriers be broken down (without our quickly rebuilding them) that we might see our truth.

Then we need to live with this truth and bring it with us in prayer, that God's word may wash over it. The revelation of God in Jesus is love. What we need to hear in the centre of our being, where our truth resides, is that 'God loves me – as I am'; this is where God's revelation becomes personal to me. This is when God's healing touch reaches out to us, and begins driving out my demons. If we leave ourselves open and exposed to God's word, in time, Lectio will eventually produce in us the harmony and consistency we seek and desire – not through repression and denial (such only mask the symptoms; they doesn't heal the wound), but through a long-term, sustained and courageous effort to eliminate whatever is incompatible with our following Christ. Our Lectio is successful if it causes us to drop our defences and allow God to touch our heart and change our life. But it all takes time – through a solid commitment to walk in Christ's way, crying out to him when we find we cannot, and then, more importantly, getting up again and having another go. Our faithfulness, shown in a long-term patience (with ourselves, as much as with God), is our expression of our belief that 'nothing is impossible to God', our expression of our hope in God's redeeming power. Our belief in God will guard us against despair; our faithfulness is the way to cultivate our hope, and growth in this hope will keep us committed.

A Simple Structure

1. Come into the Presence and call upon the Holy Spirit.

Just as we need a time and a place to work, sleep, eat, celebrate, play, meet and talk with others, so also we need a time and a place for things of the spirit and for prayer. A fixed distinct time for prayer is helpful. Prayer time is the easiest to put off; we need to give it a priority, make it happen – this IS a matter of choice. We have many things that claim our attention each day, and often these can be of great importance. But rarely do they have to be done right now, right this very minute. So, we need to give an importance to our time of prayer, by giving it a priority that is not easily overridden.

External circumstances will impact on our reading. If, for example, we do Lectio where we ordinarily work, memories of what we have done/still have to do may flow in to distract us. We need, in some way, to separate ourselves from the realm of the ordinary – if we can, a separate place for prayer is good. It can be helpful to create/build/make a sacred space and enter it by ritual – that is, doing something that puts distance between you and the 'world' (with all its tasks that belong to another time). It can be anything: perhaps just a simple prayer to start with, or something more elaborate, or it could even be going off for a walk alone. The aim is to make a place where we can be with the Lord, where we are not tugged by our passions, emotion, desires (this was what was behind the flight into the desert: to be free to do what they wanted, namely, be with God).

Further, our prayer time calls for a privacy that does not readily admit others and other distractions, where we are out of touch. Privacy is essential, for in prayer we need to be our true self in all humility and honesty (strengths AND weaknesses). We need to create this private place. In this we will need the cooperation of others – that they respect that we are generally not available at this time.

Further, noise and interruptions do disturb. What we need is a place of peace and quiet. Sometimes we can't do anything about these things, and so we will have to read here in this place/make the most of what we can do with what we've got. But if we can, we need to claim a place of peace, quiet and privacy where we can be alone with God. In this place, we need good lighting – this is a time of reading; we need to be able to read with ease, that the physical task of reading does not intrude on the time. And posture is important – if we pray in an armchair, we may relax too much; if we pray in one that is too uncomfortable, this will become the focus of our attention, and not prayer; we need a good chair. Our prayer space needs to be well aired as well – too stuffy or too warm and we will find ourselves becoming drowsy; too cold and this will be all we can think about.

Perhaps we might ...

The Bible speaks of a REAL presence, a place where we can encounter the living God whenever we will. We ought to approach it with reverence. Perhaps we might enthrone the word on a bookstand, rather than just having it on the shelf with other books. We might pick it up with real sense of awe and wonder (perhaps with a kiss), for it is the word of God, incarnate in Scripture. Such reverence will help us welcome the word and propel us into silence, enabling us to listen. For it is a recognition that we are in the presence of something greater than ourselves and before whom we should be silent. Such reverence will also help us safeguard the seriousness of what we are about, and so further aid us in maintaining the priority we give Lectio.

Perhaps we might stand or kneel to begin, remaining in that position till we are ready to begin to read the word, when we sit to do our Lectio. A mat on the floor might help mark out a space. Lighting a candle, using icons or other sacred symbols may set an atmosphere. Putting all these things out as part of a ritual in setting up may help focus the mind, to put aside our other tasks. Conversely, putting all these things away afterwards may help return us and the space to normal.

As part of our ritual entry into sacred space, it is helpful to begin by making explicit our desire to meet God. In this way, our Lectio becomes part of our search for God. This might be done through a favourite/familiar prayer, or one we compose. It is good to have some fixed prayer to start with, one that asks for help, perhaps a prayer invoking the Holy Spirit – for it was the Holy Spirit who inspired the sacred authors, and it is the same Holy Spirit who will teach us and remind us of all that Jesus has said. Simply put, we might ask the Holy Spirit to make the sacred text be for us a living communication with the Lord, and help us to understand what the Lord wants us to hear.

2. Listen to the Lord speaking through the Sacred Text.

First, we need to set aside some time each day – we have to 'make time', as opposed to 'find time'. We do this by giving Lectio a priority. This means we have to be willing to let go all our other doing for a while. Here it is better to fix a set time each day – this avoids having to decide each day when we can fit it in, and it becomes part of the auto-pilot of our daily routine. Routine has a bad press, but it actually makes life simpler. Good habits are built up by a repetition of good acts; it is easier to do the good we want to do once a habit is established. A good routine is just a set of good habits; the routine makes them happen.

In our Lectio, we need a stillness to receive God's word. We have to manage our thoughts, passions, and desires so as to be free for things of the spirit; this is part of our letting go. Here our routine (where we have built in our decision to sit with the Lord at this time and for this period) will help us, for it will have become our habit to do this now at this time. In this, the beginning of the day is more often preferred, before we are beset by the day's distractions – in this way, we don't have to rid ourselves of them before we start.

Then, Lectio is not an exercise in reading; we do not read to gather sacred knowledge. So, it is best to fix a duration/set a time period for Lectio, rather than set a fixed amount of reading to be done. The time we set each day should be do-able/realistic, so that it fits easily into our daily routine. If it's not too long, we are more likely to do it each day and be faithful to this daily encounter. Five minutes actually done each day is better than some grand plan to devote whole slabs of time that, realistically, we don't have (our Lectio will eventually develop its own momentum and bring with it a desire for more as we become more proficient at it; we can increase it later).

That said, Lectio needs a solid piece of time each day: a minimum of half an hour a day is best (we won't be able to do this every day, but we must be able to say that this is our habit). This means a sustained commitment over time and this requires effort. Further, it is good to be disciplined about the length of time we give to Lectio. We should beware the temptation to sit longer when we are having a 'good' time in prayer, just as we need to stick at it where it is not going so well and all seems dry. This all calls for a daily asceticism, a self-discipline. It requires sustained effort, but this will help produce a certain openness and a sense of leisure, both essential to Lectio. In this, our own laziness can undermine us through our unwillingness to make the required effort to do it.

The process in Lectio is simple: God speaks and we listen, then we respond. As we read, we need an affective embrace of the word; we need to be attentive to any movement of the heart. For whatever reason, a certain word or phrase will catch our attention: it will not be lights flashing and trumpets sounding, but just some mere flicker of interest – it is this we must pause over, resisting the temptation to 'move on'/keep going. It may be the first word we read that comes alive for us, or it might happen later. It is this flicker of interest we need sit with and then respond to. We need not worry about the rest of the text; there is no need to push on, it will be there tomorrow!

Thus, there is 'purposelessness' about our Lectio. We read in such a way that it may be punctuated by many such pauses; there is no set amount of reading to be done, there is nothing to be achieved. We show our reverence for the text by being willing to sit with it and listen, to figure out what it is saying (as opposed to what we want/would like it to say); we need to ponder, and be prepared to sit with what might unsettle, in a spirit of trust.

Lectio speaks to my present situation. If I'm emotional, I will see only that emotion. The Lord speaks to us where we are today. Thus, the same word can speak to us very differently on different days. Then, if I'm a newcomer (less experienced) to Lectio, I will see little (though it may be more dramatic), see less than someone more experienced. Scripture accommodates to our level of perception. This, too, will change over time, so that, in time, we will see differently, see more (hopefully); the vision gets grander. So, we may read and re-read the same book in Lectio: repetition/overexposure is not a problem. For as we come again to the Scriptures, we are not the same; we grow and change, we see/read/hear with new eyes/ears and so get a different message (and which we will not get unless we come by it again).

Our reading of Scripture is no guarantee of instant access to the fullness of revelation contained therein. There is no 'one' meaning of/in Scripture; it speaks of the mystery of God. The truth of the Bible goes beyond the discovery of the meaning of the words. Though it contains historical elements, the text is not history; it is more than that. There is a literal level, in which we can speak of its literal meaning; but there are also other levels of meaning. Apart from the literal/historical level (what happened, or seems to have happened), tradition recognises more spiritual levels of meaning (tropological: its moral teaching – here we find the text asking us to do something; allegory: its prefiguring of another mystery in things already happened – at this level we find all texts pointing us to Christ; and, anagogy: its interpretation in the light of end-time – here we get a taste of and desire for things to come, lifting our sights from the everyday to ultimate reality). These other levels of meaning may not have been intended by the author, and may not all be found in every particular text; they are the result of the Holy Spirit at work in the reader. They are a grace given to benefit the reader.

We must beware the short-sightedness of literalism, and stay open to the other levels of meaning. We have to let the Spirit speak – though there is need for discernment, for not all spirits are of God. We need to be 'playful' with the texts, give ourselves some freedom to move beyond the literal level allowing the Spirit to speak/inspire – but always with common-sense, integrity, prudence and humility. We must not be fearful of making mistakes; this will limit inspiration — always mindful that the Spirit that moved the sacred authors is also the same Spirit at work in us. A word of caution: I do not mean to say here that we are completely free to do anything we like with the text, for the authentic spiritual meanings we find in a text will be in continuity with its literal meaning and in harmony with the totality of revelation as found in Christian tradition.

... What I do

I usually try to have about four pages on the go. Why four? Four pages is about as much as I can remember as a block. I do not try to memorise the text just to be able to remember it as such, but to free me from the text so that I don't really have to read it, the text being there more as a prompt (thus I don't have to be able to recite it by heart either). Also, if nothing 'happens' during my prayer time, four pages is enough to fill my prayer time (I usually try to do about an hour early in the morning) as I slowly work my way through the pages. At the end of the four pages I usually add another sentence, having left off a sentence at the beginning.

In this way, there is a slow progress being made through the book I am reading, which at the moment is Paul's Letter to the Galatians. As I read, some word or phrase might catch my interest — and it can be the slightest thing, so that you have to be attentive; if you're not, then you just pass over and nothing happens. This is where I bring myself to the text, for it is my interest and it is triggered by something in me – it might be how I'm feeling, or something I've read, or something someone said to me, which is hooked by a word or phrase in the text. When something catches my eye, I usually write it down in my journal; I pray with a pen. This adds action/doing to sight in my experience of the word, and slows down my reading even further, and externalises it – it's not all just happening in my head. Usually by the time I have written down the sentence, another piece of Scripture comes to mind (this gets better as you become more familiar with Scripture); I write this down, too. I keep going in this way until I respond; I write this down, too.

It's important to remember that my Lectio/reading is prayer; it is not Scripture study. The pieces of Scripture I rub together might have nothing to do with one another from an exegetical point of view, and the insights I get from rubbing these together might not be the 'objective' meaning of the text intended by the author, but that's OK – it's MY prayer; it's me and God speaking. I find this process, which I find quite 'conversational, usually leads me to my prayer. I find I can end up in some rather interesting/surprising places, which I didn't know I wanted to pray about, and occasionally gain some significant insights; it really is a great way to pray. This process can take some time (and I can be surprised at how much time has passed without my noticing), so that I find I do not always get to the end of my four pages. That's OK. I can have another go tomorrow.

Sometimes, it can take a long time (don't be in a hurry to get to the end of the book) before I get to add the next sentence onto my reading. That, too, is OK; it just means that I keep reading the same material over and over again, till I have prayed it out – the monks of old used refer to Lectio as rumenatio, after what cows do when they chew their cud, chewing it over and over until there is no more goodness to be got out of it. At other times, nothing much may seem to happen and I can find myself making 'progress' through the book – perhaps a reminder to be more attentive as I read. I find this is a great way to open yourself to God's word and take it into yourself so that it becomes part of you (the word incarnate, so to speak!).

3. End with a prayer

It is good to end with a prayer. This will help to bring our session to a close, help us transit back to ordinary time/space. We might say the Lord's Prayer, or a psalm of thanksgiving, or a prayer based on what we have read, or it might be a prayer of thanks for his presence with us and for his 'word' today. It is good to take our 'word' from

Lectio with us, repeating it over and over, letting it influence our day and making the Lord present during the whole of our day. 'To listen' means 'to hear and obey': our aim is to put what we read into practice. We need to let it call and challenge us and let ourselves be converted. Or, if no word come for us, we may need to choose a word to take with us for the day, and hopefully it will work its stuff during the day, that is, lead us to prayer and contemplation.

Elements of Lectio

While to speak of Lectio it is useful to break it up into component parts, it is usually experienced as an organic whole – usually we just sit with Scriptures and meet the Lord there in his word. How much time it takes before we begin to respond depends... it just happens when it does. The whole process, given enough time, can be present in each and every period of Lectio: as we read/listen, a word strikes us (*lectio*); we let it reverberate within us, opening us, reshaping us (*meditatio*); this calls forth a response (*oratio*); finally, we rest in the Reality to which it leads us (*contemplatio*). It is not meant to be a guaranteed and ordered set of steps: 1, 2, 3, 4; prayer will come when it does. Some seem to move easily between the different 'levels', while others may take a lifetime to get there. At this moment, we may not all be capable of contemplation, but it can and will lead all to contemplation. Contemplation, that unbroken communion in wordless perpetual prayer, is the aim of Lectio. Since the time of the Desert Fathers, exposure to the word of God in Scripture is the means of achieving it.

1. Lectio/reading (listening)

First, we gather with a text to receive a word, we listen to God in his word. God speaks first, and we listen. Because God sets the agenda through the text, something external to me, it is not an exercise in naval gazing where I simply indulge my own thoughts. Lectio is a listening – letting God speak first, and then letting that word e/affect me. We do not speak first – we do not come looking for that which supports our own already existing ideals and concepts, but instead allow these to be challenged. We come seeking God – himself and nothing less; we come seeking to experience the presence of the living God – to be with him and let him be with us as he wishes to be with us. We come as we are today, with what is going on in our world today.

Lectio is not an exercise in speed-reading, so we do not just skim to pick out the essentials. Rather, Lectio is a slow savouring of the words, where we allow the text to trigger memories/associations. The emphasis is on slow. Lectio is a way of spending time with God's revealed word – it involves reflection on the meaning, applying it to one's own life situation, and a willingness to let it lead us to prayer.

Lectio is a very slow and repetitious reading. We start at the beginning and end at the end, but in between there is much meandering. Thus, we need to be prepared to stay with a particular book for a long time; it will be our constant companion for a major part of our journey. (It took me about eight years to read St Paul's Letter to the Romans!) We must beware a boredom that says, 'I'm getting nowhere'. We need to remind ourselves that our goal is not to get to the end of the book, but prayer; the book is only a vehicle.

2. Meditation (hearing)

Here we 'hold' the word (like chewing the cud) – perhaps repeating it over and over, either verbally or in the mind, till it 'descends into the heart'. This repetition, combined with the repetitious nature of the reading/Lectio itself, is of the essence of the ancient tradition of Lectio Divina. Through it we lay it down in our memory, and God's word becomes part of our very self. This is to allow the word to break us open and reform us, as in make us over/remake us. It can be helpful here to ask questions when we don't understand what is said. We don't always immediately grasp what the word is saying to us, especially if it is at odds with our habitual way of perceiving things. An initial response, when we don't understand, is just to persevere in it, not lightly dismissing anything just because it doesn't make sense/is contradictory/whatever – leave it sit there as a question; we will eventually get an answer/gain insight.

A danger, though, is in getting caught up in our own thoughts, desires and insights. Lectio can be very satisfying, leading us to wonderful ideas and inspirations and great insights. But if we're not willing to leave these, we will not get to contemplation. Lectio is not about thoughts, ideas and insights, but about being with the Lord. Rather, what we are looking/listening for here is any response in us, the result of our affective embrace of the word. We need to let our feeling get involved; Lectio is more than just intellectual stimulation. We are meeting with God; we need feeling to relate – with anyone, and so also with God. It is this that calls forth our response that we want to share as we move into prayer.

Here it is good to remind ourselves of how artificial these divisions are for one flows into the other in an organic way. It is in our reading (*lectio*) that some word of phrase catches our attention. It is in pausing over this word or phrase and chewing it over (*meditation*) that our affective side gets involved. As it becomes clearer what is our desire, so it turns into prayer (*oration/response*), where we tell God how we feel, what we want or need to do. Then having disclosed ourselves in all honesty, we are free to just sit with this One with whom we can be and have been most intimate (*contemplation*). They process might start unfolding on the first word of our Lectio, or on the last, or... perhaps not at all – and then we might find that, later in the day, we make some connection with what we've read and so caught up in the wonder of it all.

3. Oration (responding)

During our Lectio something causes us to pause, meditate. This meditation then calls forth a response: thanksgiving, praise, petition, repentance, adoration. This is our prayer. (Writing out our prayer may be useful later as a closing prayer, and/or to take with us in the rest of our day to recall our experience in Lectio.) We can see here how Lectio precedes prayer. In this way, the initiative is with God, for it is his word (Scripture) that opens the conversation with us, and to which we are called to respond.

As we read, we need to be attentive to any movement in our heart and indulge the feeling: we may be pierced to the heart, or moved to tears of sorrow or joy, or just aroused by the smallest flicker of interest – don't worry about/be afraid of what or where these may lead, but just let the prayer come, let it speak whatever it might be. The word may speak directly to our situation, producing feelings of compunction – speak from here. Or the word may evoke a feeling – sit with it till you become conscious of what is your desire and offer this. Or our reading may inspire in us a desire for reform/greater endeavour – pray this.

Note: we pray all the way through this process — when we open our book, settle our minds, as we read and ponder. Here we mean the particular prayer to which our Lectio now leads us. Lectio (the reading part) is not an exercise in itself – it's supposed to lead to prayer. Lectio is God's word to us; it begins a conversation in which God speaks first and we are called to make a response (perhaps we might say 'considered' response, to account for the meditation aspect – though I hesitate here, for I would in no way wish diminish or impair our spontaneity or to imply an intellectual process at the expense of the affective, for here we are speaking about matters of the heart).

Our Lectio-meditation should be a process that is repeatedly interrupted by prayer (these days, more often than not, I usually find I have one big interruption, in which it takes me all my Lectio time to find my way to my prayer, what it was that first caused me to pause in the first place; this is perhaps why it takes me so long to read even a short epistle). If no prayer comes (perhaps we are going through a dry period), then we can insert a prayer – for example, if our inability to pray frustrates us and leaves us feeling like we are wasting our time, offer that to God and ask his help. Or, perhaps we might see each verse as a prayer addressed to God and as coming out of our life, and simply praying that. Using Scripture in this way will help us engage/get back in touch with our desire for prayer.

4. Contemplation (resting)

Lectio leads us to contemplation, by way of meditation and prayer. This is just a 'being with' the Lord, after all the emotion is spent, a sitting there together in silence with no need to say anything, just abiding with God in his Temple in stillness and quiet. This is union with God, but is often accompanied by or experienced/felt as a union with all creation. Lectio leads to contemplation, but in so doing it becomes an initiation into solidarity with all humanity. As we draw nearer to God, we will also find a harmony within ourselves. Thus, we can understand how our encounter with the word leads us to reform our deeds; it is our seeking to manifest this harmony (our union with God, others, ourselves) in all that we do. This is the fruit/flowering of Lectio — where, in our prayer, we become the subject of Christ's prayer (this is what he wants us to do/what we are led to want to do); where, in our living, Christ, with whom we are now one, becomes the do-er of our actions (these are but two sides of the one coin).

Note: not all Lectio periods will lead to this. For some this might come readily and often; for others it might take a whole lifetime – but it will happen.

Some Other Ways of Doing Lectio

There is no one way to do Lectio. Each person will need to develop their own style.

The Elements method

We can use the elements of Lectio, given above, as the basis of a structure for our Lectio. We begin by reading the passage through once to get an overview of the text, and then again but this time noting any words or phrases that stand out – these we try to remember. Then we read the text again, pausing to reflect on what God is asking of us here, what God is saying to us here. Is God consoling me? Or challenging me? Or inspiring me? And over what... my relationship with him? With another or others? With myself? Again, we read the text but this time pausing to consider our response to the God who has just spoken to us; this is our prayer. We might ask for help, for ourselves, or for another/others. We might give thanks, or seek forgiveness, or express our desire to do something. Or we might just want to give praise. Then we read the text one more time, but this time not to do anything but sit in God's presence – not speaking; just being with. When ready we finish with a prayer, perhaps the Our Father.

Divine Office method

Another way to Lectio is to copy the structure of the Divine Office: an opening prayer, 'O God, come to my assistance; O Lord make haste to help me'. Then some Psalmody to help us quieten the mind (to say psalms meaningfully, we have to put aside all our cares, etc., thus freeing ourselves to be open to listen), enter the sacred space, come into God's presence. A reading – if a word speaks, need to stay with that word, rather than push on to finish the reading; sit with it till it draws forth a response, which will form our prayer. Note: the Liturgy of the Hours is cyclical; the reading will return again next year, so if we don't finish today, there is always next year!

Centring Prayer method

This is a highly abbreviated style.

The method begins with a movement of faith – that God will be present with me. Then we recall a word from memory (*lectio*). In this type of prayer, the word needs to be short – as recommended in *The Cloud of Unknowing*. Often the same word is used each time. Perhaps: 'I am with you always'; 'The Kingdom is within you'; 'The Father and I will make our home with you'; 'Be still and know that I am God'. We let this word be present to us by repetition (*meditation*). Then we respond with a movement of love (*oration*). Finally, we let this love come to rest at the Centre (*contemplation*).

Levels of Meaning method

Here we read the text attentively, to understand its meaning literally. Then, as we meditate on it, we seek to contextualise it within the totality of God's revelation. This text relates to Christ, the end-point/high-point of revelation, and places this Christ before us. Then we apply it to our life: How does it affect me? What are its practical implications for me? What is this Christ asking me to do?

Our answer is our response to the word in the text. Then we let this nourish our prayer: this is what I want to do. This arouses our desire, which is ultimately our desire for union with the God who inspired the text... and here we are invited to rest. Afterwards, we take our prayer with us through the day, that it might become real in all that we do; thus does it bear fruit.

Some Difficulties

Some days, his word will speak, other days not and the words remain just words. Sometimes, we may experience his presence as a terrible absence. Some days, he just doesn't show. So, we speak of dryness and 'dark night'. Our initial experience of this especially (following on the heels of our first fervour for this type of prayer, during which God's word seemed fresh and alive and near) can feel like something has gone wrong; we can easily become discouraged. But it doesn't mean that God is not present – we might recall, for instance, the Footprints poem. Nor does it mean that we cannot try to understand (a danger here is that we turn Lectio into an exercise in seeking meaning). Here in this drought, what we are actually learning is a humility that has us wait on God and submit to his ways.

To break this cycle, if our spell of dryness continues for some time, it may be helpful to just jot down a word and try free association, especially with other Scriptural texts, and see where it leads – here the more familiar we are with Scripture, the better this will work. Or we may need to look at and renew our commitment: 'Yes, this is what I want to do'. The effectiveness of God's word is dependent on our own subjective dispositions; the word needs to fall on receptive soil. In any event, we need to remain faithful, hang in there, sit in the silence and wait for the Lord; in time the desert will bloom.

If the spell of dryness continues for some time, to just soldier on is not always helpful. It is good to look at our situation and try to figure out why. Why does God not show? Why does the text not speak? We are searching for God. That means that we have not yet found him – thus there should always be a feeling of 'not-quite-yet'-ness about our endeavour. His seeming absence should remind us of our need to keep looking, rather than be an opportunity to entertain temptations to give up. Then, sometimes the text is just obscure; that it doesn't speak is not our fault – we may have to work really hard to get meaning out of some texts. Biblical texts were written long ago, by different people for different reasons using different styles and different languages: sometimes the meaning is just not clear.

Then, too, it is not normal to experience God every time we read, where God seems to seize us/the blinding flash/moved to conversion/made new again; this is not the norm. Further, sometimes God is just silent. This could mean just that we are not ready yet to hear, and so we are left to ourselves for the moment. From time to time, we need a new way of seeing, so we have to abandon our old way of seeing and we are 'blinded', so to speak, before we can put it together in a new way and see anew. In the transition we see nothing. Then again, as we grow we change, which will change the way we pray. What worked yesterday, may not work today. If this state continues, it may be an invitation to seek a new way to pray. Or God's absence may just simply be because God is mystery – sometimes we just can't penetrate. What all this means is that we will have periods of silence; expect them, and don't be discouraged by them.

More often, though, the cause is in us; fix this up and the text will begin to speak again. External noise can fill up all our inner space, shutting out any possibility for contemplation, so that we do not/cannot notice any inner movements of the heart, shutting out all possibility for contemplation. Sometimes, it is outside our control; other people can be noisy. Sometimes, there is not much we can do about it (apart from shutting the door of our room), but we do have some control over the noise we make. Even soft music, lovely as it is, can inhibit us here, filling up our silence. We need to learn to sit quietly, without even the radio on in the background. Here we might find that, at first, we can't handle the silence – like children afraid in the dark; as a child who wants to have a night-light on, so we compulsively want some background noise. Such noise can be addictive, like a child's security blanket. We need to learn to be comfortable in the silence; this can only be done through experience.

When first experienced, silence can be troubling. It can seem just like some vast void. There our own dark/deeper thoughts emerge; this can be frightening. But it is only in our silence that we become aware of what is going on in us. We need to become familiar with our self, see our self as we are, and so not have to run away scared or ashamed. In prayer, we need to be totally honest; we have to stand naked before our God. If we cannot stand to be naked/honest with our self, we certainly won't be able to do so before God. Here the call is to know our self, to become used to our self in this deep place, so that all our self-rejections and all that drives us may not force us to retreat.

Then it can be that our own internal noise might prevent us from listening: cares and concerns from our work, in our relation-ships, whatever, keep playing over and over in our minds. If we are dissatisfied with our lot, we may find ourselves daydreaming about alternatives, or find ourselves constantly going over and over our catalogue of grievances. All these intrude on our reading. We have to learn how to set aside our thoughts, feelings, and other distrac-tions, else we cannot pray. In *The Cloud of Unknowing*, the author recommends, when we find we cannot set our inner thoughts and distractions aside, that we just acknowledge this and offer it up as our prayer, asking the Lord to deliver us from our bondage. Thus, even our distractions, if we cannot be free of them, we can turn into an opportunity for prayer.

Or then again, sometimes we are just not in a state where we can hear. We might be ill physically, which will restrict our ability to sit and listen. Here we just have to do the best we can. Sometimes we are troubled with drowsiness. This may be physical. We need to recognise that there are limits to what we can do. We should choose a time when we're less tired, and have a well-aired space which is not too warm. Our posture should not be too relaxed, and we should have a limit to our time. But then again, our tiredness might be something else. Sleepiness can be a form of passive resistance – we need to ask the question. Odd occasions are OK, but if regular, we need to look into it/do something about it.

Sometimes, we will be unable to settle for any length of time; we can't sit still, and are restless, jumpy, unable to pay attention, unable to commit to any serious, sustained activity. This is a problem to do with commitment. We feel we should be/would prefer to be doing something (perhaps, anything) else. If we can't settle, we can't hear. The ancients called this *acedia*, and the remedy is: 'stay in your cell' – just admit what's going on, and sit with the discomfort; it will pass. We might not seem to achieve anything by staying put, but in so doing we reassert control over ourselves so that WE determine what we are doing, rather than being driven by this 'spirit' of acedia.

Sometimes, we can become oppressed by busyness. Yes, urgent things do need to be done, but for the most part they do not need to be done now at this moment and so can be deferred to a later time — perhaps we might just make a note of them if can't put them out of mind, with a promise to attend to them at another more suitable time. And perhaps we need to remind ourselves that we have given Lectio a priority. We need to learn by doing not to budge too easily from this serious business (that is, our Lectio). The more we refuse to move, the less we are plagued by the other matters of lesser priority.

Aligned with this, we need to avoid turning Lectio into what it is not. It is not study time, so we refuse to let our Lectio become a time for Scripture study. It is not a time for preparing for homilies or teaching, so we do not go off chasing down a good insight making it more marketable that may be useful elsewhere. Lectio is a quiet, repetitive exercise. If we become too intellectually busy, it slips away as a more active study of the text takes over, where I become self-absorbed. Lectio is about relationship, about conversation; one cannot converse with another who is preoccupied.

Then again, the reason that we are unable to pray may have to do with our neighbour. If we fall out with our neighbour, we can't spurn God in our neighbour and then expect to meet him in prayer. Our disharmony will impact on our prayer. We may need to attend to some area of charity, or justice, or obedience/co-operation, that we have refused to resolve, or have rationalised away, or allowed to just sit there while we do nothing. We need at least to recognise any wrongdoing on our part, and try to make amends if we find any. If we find none, we must try to find in our hearts the will to forgive, rather than just nurse the hurt for this will surely consume us. Practically, forgiveness means absorbing the hurt, rather than trying to get even or passing it on/dumping it on another. Where we find reconciliation is not possible, we may just simply have to let our grievance go, recognise our own powerlessness in this matter and hand it over to him who is all-powerful. Finally, it might be that what God is saying to us, we just don't want to hear – it is a kind of deafness on our part.

What to Read?

This gets down to personal choice: what attracts you? There is no right choice, but we must be prepared for going a long way with a long-term companion. We are seeking God, seeking salvation. In a real sense, we don't know the way, so we have to seek guidance and take it on trust that it will lead us to where we wish to go, and we must be willing to be led there. This means there is a risk involved, and we are vulnerable in this. Care, then, needs to be taken in the choice of what we read, to protect us in our openness, which is the openness of a disciple to a master. We need to be sure that it is God who is speaking to us, that it is God who is leading us.

Bible

The Bible is sacred reading par excellence. Any book of the Bible is God's word; all are suitable. For us Christians, Christ is to be found in the Gospels, the Gospels as situated in the context of the New Testament, and the New Testament in context of Old Testament. In a real sense, then, every page of Scripture speaks of Christ. Then, too, Scripture reveals/unfolds God's plan of salvation, and so all of it leads us to Christ; we can start reading it anywhere (see John 5:39-40). Any part of the Bible is suitable for a disciple of Christ. But it does mean, though, that we who are seeking to meet Christ in the Scriptures, have to read them in the light of his resurrection, we need an Easter perspective – though not an Easter without its Good Friday (see Luke 24:27).

Some use

• THE GOSPELS. These are best, at least initially, for we are attempting to get to know our Lord Jesus Christ, and he is most easily recognisably present in them. Having worked through a Gospel, some then like to alternate a reading of the Old Testament with a reading of the New Testament, or a Gospel with an Epistle, as a way of getting to know the word more broadly, more fully.

• FAVOURITE PASSAGES. But our familiarity with them may mean that we do not see anything 'new' in the text, and so we are not moved into unexpected territory (entry into the new and unexpected is part of the 'adventure' of Lectio). So, we are not challenged to see, for we only see the same familiar landscape. It is in being open to the unfamiliar, the difficult, and the challenging found in the fullness of Revelation, that we are steadily moved away from our prejudices, our closed convictions, our ideologies, towards a wholeness that transcends our present narrow worldview.

• SOME BIBLES SUGGEST PASSAGES FOR DIFFERENT OCCASIONS, DIFFERENT MOODS. Here we might find the comfort we seek, for example, if we are lonely or sad, but this is not what Lectio is about. It leaves us in charge – it is really we who speak first: 'Give me a word of comfort'. Sometimes, when we are feeling in some way vulnerable/in need, it could be that this might be just what is needed to let the Lord speak the word we need to hear; it is better to let the Lord speak first.

• SOME LIKE A RANDOM SELECTION. However, care is needed here to avoid a temptation to superstition over 'God having chosen this word for me'. Simply put: the word which 'opens' for us is not an answer to some question. Then, too, the randomly selected reading is taken out of context and so we may end up with the wrong message.

• SOME USE THE READINGS FOR THE DAY IN THE LITURGY. This helps to improve our participation in the Liturgy, and the passage chosen is not my choice (that is, it is not me who speaks first). But again, these selections are out of context, and we may need to supplement our reading here. A problem here can be that there is a new text every day – sometimes we need to sit with a word/phrase for some time to hear what it is saying; we need to be able to stay with a word for as long as our fascination remains. This is not to say that a text cannot/will not move us. It is just to note that an element of Lectio, that slow and leisurely reading, might be at risk here. Then, too, we need to mindful that not all of Scripture is covered in the Church's Scriptural cycle.

• LECTIO CONTINUA: this is reading a chosen Book of the Bible right through from beginning to end. Some like to choose a Book according to the liturgical season: Isaiah for Advent; Jeremiah for Lent; Lamentations for Holy Week; Epistle of John for Easter Time (though this, too, might limit the time we have to read a book).

Lectio Continua is probably the preferred method. Reading random selections takes the passage out of context. Often, due to the limitation inherent in translations, we only get a feel for the true meaning of the words as we expose ourselves to the whole message the sacred author is trying to convey. Reading the Book right through from beginning to end will thus help prevent the misunderstandings that can arise in taking parts of it out of context. Similarly, in reading the whole book through, we open ourselves to the whole message – those bits we like and so which are not troublesome,

AND, more importantly, those bit we don't like, those bits which challenge us, those bits which would move us to where we would prefer not to go.

These challenge us to let go of our prejudices, our fixed beliefs, and our settled ways of behaviour. Thus do we grow; thus are we moved towards wholeness and holiness. Thus do we avoid the pitfalls associated with selectivity, which may allow us to avoid the challenges, allow us to stay where we are, through our choosing only those passages we like, those passages which support and confirm us in our set views and fixed ways. Further, our reading is not to get to some core message — the guts of it, its essence – as though the rest of it is then of less value. All of it is God's word; God can and does and will speak through any of it and all of it. We cannot afford to quickly pass over any of it just because we judge it to be not the essential message. Lectio is not skimming over the text, reading bits, leaving out those which are obscure/difficult/unfamiliar – such a way of reading will not encourage us to stay with Lectio, for we will soon find ourselves bored.

Not every text will speak, but this doesn't justify restricting what we read – we will be surprised by just what does speak. Choice of a Book will get down to some personal attraction for that Book, but once chosen, stick with that Book till we've prayed it right through. If we come up against a brick wall, we persevere in trust – the choice was made in good faith; it will bear fruit. Sometimes it may be that we're just not ready to hear at this moment and need more time to hear. So, we re-read and chew it over – that's our part in it. Meanwhile, the word works away on us steadily, softening our heart till at last it begins to open – then we will hear. This takes time; we have to persist in faith.

Other Material

• LECTIO, and here we are speaking of Lectio Divina and not a wider more general spiritual reading, need not be restricted to the Bible. But we do recognise the Bible as THE inspired word of God – it is here that we will most readily hear the word of God. However, there is truth (the word is truth) in other traditions, and in other spiritual writings. Lectio is a way of reading that suspends critical faculty; we need to read without discernment, without the need to verify the truth (it is more about relationship with the truth, than about finding the truth) of what we read. For this reason, we need to be careful in our choice of what we read. We need to read that which is consistent with/contains the truth, that which expresses the perennial faith of our Church.

• CHURCH TRADITION represents the collective interpretation of the truth, gathered over the centuries; that which is consistent with it is more likely to be true. A reading, then, from such as the Office of Readings is quite suitable, as are liturgical texts and the writings of the Fathers/Mothers of the Church, the Doctors of the Church, and some of the mystics, as well as the official documents of the Church, such as Council texts and encyclicals. For those following his Rule, St Benedict recommended biblical commentaries of renowned and Orthodox Catholic Fathers, as well as the writings of Monastic Fathers such as John Cassian (his Institutes and probably his Conferences), and also the Rule of St Basil. Others can profitably use these as well.

• GOD IS ALSO PRESENT in creation, in the beauty of the arts, and in people. It is possible to do Lectio through all of these media.

Conclusion

'Listen carefully, my son/my daughter, to the Master's instruction, and attend to them with the ear of your heart. This is advice from a father who loves you; welcome it, and faithfully put it into practice' (*The Rule of St Benedict*, The Prologue:1). These words open *the Rule of St Benedict*. They capture and sum up the disciple's stance: we are to listen to what the Master has to say, welcome it, and then do it. This essentially is what we are about in Lectio Divina: listening to God's word, taking it into ourselves, and then letting it influence our behaviour.

In the Scriptures we do hear God speaking. Quoting the Psalm, Benedict urges us, 'If today you hear his voice, harden not your heart', adding 'The Lord waits for us daily to translate into action, as we should, his holy teaching' (*The Rule of St Benedict*, The Prologue:10, 35). Most of us, in our deepest self, do desire to do what is good and right. Alas! We are more like Julian of Norwich's servant, in her parable of 'A Lord and His Servant', who runs off eagerly to do his lord's will... but quickly falls headlong into a ditch, from which he cannot rise (Julian of Norwich, *Revelations of Divine Love*. Long Text 51). It is as St Paul notes: we want to do good, but we do not (indeed cannot) do it! (Romans 7:19).

Calling it a 'battle', Benedict knows the task he has in mind for us will be difficult: 'We must prepare our hearts and mind for the battle of holy obedience to his instructions'. So, he advises, 'What is not possible to us by nature, let us ask the Lord to supply by help of his grace' (*The Rule of St Benedict*, The Prologue: 40-41) – much of our prayer in Lectio will be given over to lamenting our inability. Covering a full spectrum of emotions, from frustration and anger to disappointment and despair, our prayer will come down to St Paul's realisation: 'Miserable man that I am! Who will rescue me from this body of death?' (Romans 7:24). We will be tempted to give it all away: I can't do this! Benedict just gently counsels, 'Do not be daunted immediately by fear and run away from the road that leads to salvation. It's bound to be narrow at the outset. But as we progress in this way of life and in faith, we shall run on the path of God's commands, our hearts overflowing with the inexpressible delight of love.' (*The Rule of St Benedict*, The Prologue:48-49) It is a Way we can go; we will get there if we but have a go. Our is to believe that God can do this in us. (Romans 4:18ff) For our Lectio to bear its fruit in us we are going to need faith and perseverance.

It is precisely this, however, that we are to learn in the battle of holy obedience: that we can't do it. Wisely, Benedict has included in his Rule a small chapter on *The Assignment of Impossible Tasks*. There he urges us to have a go, while at the same time admitting our inability. Benedict's way is a way of humility. Our Lectio will bring us to an honest appraisal of ourselves, which will be painful at times. But it is here in this place that we do finally open ourselves to the workings of God's Holy Spirit. Under its influence, we will find we will start to do the good we want to do. There, knowing ourselves fully, we will at once recognise the Lord's hand at work in us and this will be cause for great rejoicing. Our Lectio, too, will have periods of great joy. This is its promise.

Lectio is a great adult way to pray. It can and will draw us to grow and mature, till at last we reach an integrity that will let us stand once more naked before our Lord, as we once did in the Garden of Paradise, without shame but truly in all honesty/humility: Here I am, Lord! This we have come for; this we are made for: to be at home with our God.

May God richly bless you on your journey into life with him.